TREE

TREBLE POETS 3

Gordon Symes
Janet Harrison
Philip Crick

1977

CHATTO & WINDUS

LONDON

Published by
Chatto & Windus Ltd
42 William IV Street
London WC2N 4DF

*

Clarke, Irwin & Co. Ltd.
Toronto

Acknowledgements are due to the editors of
the following periodicals, in which some of
the poems in this book first appeared: *Ambit,
Caret, Countryman, Critical Quarterly, Delta,
English, Iron, Meridian, New Headland, New
Humanist, New Measure, New Poetry, New
Statesman, Oasis, Outposts, Samphire, Tlaloc,
Transcript, Twentieth Century*, University of
Houston *Forum, Yankee.*

British Library Cataloguing in Publication Data

Symes, Gordon
    Gordon Symes — Janet Harrison —
    Philip Crick. — (Treble poets; 3).
    ISBN 0-7011-2212-9
    1. Harrison, Janet 2. Crick, Philip
    821'.9'1408 PR1225
    English poetry

Printed in Great Britain by
Redwood Burn Ltd.
Trowbridge & London

CONTENTS

Philip Crick

GORDON SYMES

OG POWER

Og the ugly ogre, with his huge bed,
The ghost of a shadow of a memory
Left behind like greyish stains
The churches never quite rubbed out, odd snags
Of language, place names sticking like tar
(Aweful Aughaval, obscure Ogbury),
Occurrent Og rivers, a prehistoric giant daubed
On Hoggar rocks, garblings of Og-god
Reverberating from Ireland to Haiti
(Unremembered every Hogmanay), a runic
Alphabet called Ogham, incidences
Of sacred hogs and oaks, leading back to

Og the First, like an agile bulbed spider
Laying across the world his tough threads
Of sea-power, mining know-how and dogma,
His brightskinned argonauts long before Christ
Dawning on America from the east,

Assigning scratch farmers and superstitious folk
To ages of Ogs or Agas,
New ecologies of metals and worths,
Wrought gardens of seedless jewels, golden boughs,
Granaries of stones, art galleried
From mountainous labours, perfection's image
And hunger still clutching on the breath —
Kingdoms of Ugh and Ah.

AN EXPLORER

I think that Mungo Park,
Who didn't discover the Niger's
Course but how much he could stand
Of indignity, loss, fatigue,

Typifies questing man
More tellingly than most explorers.

Timbuctoo, Eldorado, always
Have one more goal in the way.
What he went to Africa for
Became just keeping on
Being tested for something else.

His ordeals seem low-keyed.
(I don't mean they weren't hard.)
An air of sour farce overhangs.
Cruel kings had comic names
Like Daisy and Tiggity Sego.
Women thought his nose funny,
Wanted him to take his clothes off.
He kept losing things. Even death,
Which often came quite close, was often
Put off by something trivial,
As if not caring all that much.
Once, a small pig saved him.

Or, think of him a captive
At the court of king Ali (court?
Scruffy tents, smelling of camel):
How, nearly off his head with thirst,
He crawled half a mile towards
Lowing sounds (must mean well);
The herdsman, worried about pollution,
Tipped a bucket in the cattle trough.
Look at the pilgrim now,
Kneeling at the fount of life
Slobber for slobber with the cows.

He did meet with some kindness —
From women, as you would expect.

How single-minded he was, though.
If he passed, almost blindly, tests,

He was blind to much more,
To the no heart of darkness.
He had not come to judge or help,
But to find which way a river went.
Praising God, he kept his pity dry.
Slaves in chain gangs, diseases,
Were noted by him in passing.

But whether he really thought
To reach port (as his last letter
To his wife was bound to say) —
Whether, when truth struck, a surge
Of knowing that not himself but
Someone would drive the river home
Buoyed him, or lead weight
Of all's waste took him under,
That day on Bussa rapids,
Or even if it was at Bussa,
Is uncertain. Like the Niger ending
In a delta. Like most quest endings.

AN ORIENTAL MEMENTO

A memory (he said) came back, and comes: the steep hill
Above Kailana, how it dazingly clung
To the blind feet of women overhung
With hay trusses as though they were thatched. It still
Clings to him, sometimes with the prickle of a smell
Of — sandalwood, curing skins, burning dung?
Whatever, real; he meant, as vaguely strong
As something smells when you started to become ill.
Is he ill? How? Not, he thought, with wanting to return.
If anything, he hated it there. And half hated
Himself now, for this feeling he can't exorcise.
Is he their father and brother? Or how implicated
With the shadowy shrill children at every turn
Plaguing him like flies, and dying like flies?

WORLDS APART

(Ses ailes de géant l'empêchent de marcher – Baudelaire, 'L'Albatros')

They are, really, quite separate worlds:
The clean sweep of an imagined
Comity of love and crafts,
And the ways we actually live
Or would live, even if well led.

That world simply mirrors There,
Not what we do at best here.
Our gains are just more of the same.
But Utopias are not staffed
By any of the people we know.

Pointless, then, invoking – not
The albatross, which I haven't seen –
Say, this woodpigeon's crass dodder
And grab, after so fluently
Mating the air, purely gliding.

No analogy. It is still air's lover,
A bit awkward, eating on land;
We are still dreaming about escaping.
But we could learn from monkeys
(Not the ones we capture and spoil)

Whose intense fondness, moony spells,
Nitpicking and gawping lust,
Whose graceful giving place,
Rejection of technology,
Come all of a piece.

UNIVERSAL UNCLE

You get to know him when you are quite young.
He is your first intimation that the world
Is not all father and mother. He is something like father,
But it's the difference that intrigues and charms.
He never lays down the law, doesn't overpower
Like mother, who sometimes seems as though she could eat
   you.
He appears unexpectedly, often with a present.
His presents are more exciting than father's, which are
Not quite what you wanted and are meant to do you good.
It is he who will take you on your first visit
To the brothel — who will teach you toughnesses
That parents come to expect without explaining why.
Though he was never there to help with dull homework.

It's not clear what he does. You detect a guardedness
Like the memory of an old family quarrel
Between him and father. They don't really get on.
You gather he had an accident once — a bad fall.
It's not much talked about. Was he drunk at the time?
It would fit that interestingly world-weary air.
(If there was an aunt, she was even more mysterious.
Did she have a name something like Lilian?)

In retrospect, though, he would often promise treats
That never materialised. As you grow older,
His charm rather fades. You hardly notice when he finally
Dies (of that fall?). Or you sense for a moment
That perhaps he was lonely and disappointed.
You may have mattered to him more than you thought.
He may leave you something in his will.

HERACLES

This would be a suitable time,
Men being conspicuous for
Their growth in physique and folly,
To celebrate natural man's hero
Heracles. Who once propped up heaven.
Heaven, grudging him its need,
Repaid him mad fits. His ham fists
Ran with the blood of his children.

Breaking was what he was good at:
Heads, records, wild beasts, wind,
New ground. The stories send him shouldering
Over frontiers, smashing and clearing.
Strength mattered. His pythons of muscles,
Trees of calves, were fleshed out
By fear in its own image.

Fantasy too had a hand,
Supplying him whole bullocks to gorge,
Tuns of wine to gulp. Barrel belly
Bolsters our secret hate of reason,
And day-dream exempts from surfeit. He mounted
And managed fifty goggling
Virgins in a single night.

There was more to him than that.
One story made him vote
For Miss Virtue, not her randy sister.
But that idyll never seemed to fruit.
If he went on tipping libations
To the hearth goddess, his bones always knew
He was not going to settle —

Haunted by children crying,
By madness hanging round the corner;
At home (which was anywhere he might be)

To a call from the king's messenger
With another labour to pay
For his sins – well, for something more
Driving him to look for labours.

In the end he was made god,
God of men learning to be civil.
Sea traders were first to adopt him.
He had charge of goods, money, the home
(Who never had one). And, though in his time
An easy swearer, was named
For sealing bargains and pledges.

We might name him today,
Who have eaten and drunk too well
And now are worried by children's voices
And thinking we hear Somebody's tread
Thump like a clock coming closer
With another penance to pay.
We may need your giant's guts soon,
Heracles, your jumbo submissiveness.

LOVE POETRY

The amorous poems of Propertius,
Though turned and fettled
Sweatily with a gutfelt skill
Our nerves twang to, are mostly run of the mill
Amorous poems. Yes, we know all about that
Embracing like strangling, tangle of longing to

Be one be free. And his relish of
Hurting – *in love I want to feel pain
Or listen to it; yours or mine,
Tears must flow* – kinky it may be, -
Is all part of the whole boiling where
Masses of young verses still get stewed.
15

At vos incertam is marvellous, of course,
Especially the last lines. But *only*
A lover knows when and by what
Death he shall die is only
A grander way of saying
'Dear God, how I want you'.

Sometimes, though, you surprise
A different note from him; its pang
Stays longer. *With you — or for you —*
I shall always be fighting, nor
Where you are care about rest. Or
For you — *aut pro te.* Oh yes,

This is love poetry. Yes, this,
When the tongueing, when nail and tooth
Devour themselves, touches closest to
Tears. (As if, almost, he was saying
Even then, as some think he did later,
'Dear God, how I want *You*'.)

LET ME INTO HERE

Swinging, he hit the glass a terrible blow.
It never flinched. The axe fell out of his hands.
The images kept on walking still,
Talking in twos and agreeing without any sounds.

MALLARMÉ'S THREE TOMBS

Mallarmé, haunted by paper's impenetrable
White, space's blue void, interchanging between
The real and the word, Mallarmé, orchestrator
Of absences, seriously attended to
Graves or monuments of the writers he most
Trusted. It seemed a way of making sure
They were somewhere else. But here and now,
Still this side of the space-thick paper,
Was where their dying engraved them; him too.

1. Poe

What he was to himself he becomes for ever
Now: poet. With a bared blade now he stings
A shocked age into seeing what they should have seen,
That it was death having his say, that strange tone.

They reared uglily a one-necked monster of heads
Against heaven's courier bringing back a purer sense
Of what their words could mean. They howled the oracles
Down — said it was the demon drink talking.

If hardfaced earth and cloud desolatingly yield
Nothing our insight now can artifice in relief
To soften the bald glare of Poe's monument —

Calm outcrop of what unknowable eruption —
At least let this granite signify 'No further'
To the flights of blackener words and 'Be scarcer'.

2. Baudelaire

The buried temple, the street drain, disgorges from its
Tomb of mouth frothing mud and rubies

A presence of the underworld — Anubis,
All his muzzle on fire with madly barking.

Now: see how the lamp wick is twisted by oil's
Bad breath; how it picks up dirt like insults;
How uncouthly it still perfects light's pubic emblem.
It's the lamp's bias makes the flame seem out of true.

No wreathed leaves drying for city's want of evening
Could conjure such blessing as now comes to settle
Over against impressionlessly marble Baudelaire

(There not there in every shiver of night's veil)
His own ghost essence — a sovereign poison
Which we still have to breathe if it kills us.

3. Verlaine

Bitterly the black slab resists the wind's heave but
Won't be stopped now — not by devout hands
Dwelling on its likeness to man's hard lot
As if with a blessing on — what? Birth's death-mask?

Here almost always when ringdoves roocoo
These ghostly mourners smother in embraces like
Clouds the fruit-sheen of the star future.
But one sparkle would mint new folk like silver.

Has anyone followed this far his solitary caper
(The footloose trail earths here) in search of
Verlaine? He's hidden in the grass, Verlaine,

With his only finding — and quite simply accepting,
Neither drinking nor holding back his breath —
A shallow rivulet, not what they called death.

O N E   E Y E

One-eye bright
Gave the old folk a fright
Glaring them down
Banging on the skylight
Keeping them going going gone.

One-eye, north sky father,
Traded in the other
For a drink of wisdom. He knew
Wise would see further than two.

One-eye, nightmare of the Celts,
Kept the other closed — or else.
Enemies and crops, they said,
Would shrivel if he lifted that lid.

One-eye the monster Polypheme
(Relic of a lost regime?)
Never had but one
And could be imposed on.

One-eye down the ages
Peers out of fiction's bogeys,
Black patching inner eye lack.
(Eliot found him in a Tarot pack.)

One-eye reigned
In countries of the blind.
'Daylight robbers', said science
Sizing down gods and giants.

'One-eye is dead',
The true visionaries said.
'Let justice be seen — will be done'.
But where are the two-eyed men?

One eye on the main chance
Or in a keyhole trance
Or at a new viewfinder
Or bringing down a star
Or narrowed to a lab slide
Or straining over a bomb sight

One-eye bright
Switching on the night.

G. S. L O V E D S. S.

How I took to heart
The gall and ruth
Of Stevie Smith,
Who confronted not-God
With reproach unloud,
Who handled fearful myth
Like the washing up.

She scaled really bad times
To a manageable truth
Of schoolgirl rhymes.
Her way of keeping faith
With outraged feeling,
Or to shame deadly sloth,
Was singing about and drawing
Real animals, lost dollies.
From where most people stood,
Her by herself singing
May have sounded cracked. I found
It full of consoling.

S L A T E

Pressures we can hardly imagine pressed
Slates out of mountains; changed shales and mudstones
With upheave and sideshift, overheating, overcrowding,
Packing down ironed flat stacked
Layers of splittable plates, clean slates.

An old church roof's metallic bloom
In London suddenly lit up this recall
Of slate country: how these bleak flakes,
Planed slivers of not quite rock or stone,
Showered across the border from Wales,
Uncolouring childhood. Their meanings were grey.
Getting slated was miserable. Poverty's shame
Was put on the slate. The word itself
Slices and grates. Skreekings of slate
Pencils still meant school then.
Slates were what Moses wrote on and smashed
Like an angry schoolmaster. The school,
Every cottage and outhouse, was closed over
With their monochrome. They were genteelly named
For sizes — Queen, Marchioness, Small Lady.
But could be wickedly dangerous in gales,
Like flying axe-blades.

                    In memory now they seem
To lie about everywhere, under hedges,
In garden patches, beds of ditches.
Dead buildings shed them like feathers.
They stuck out of paths edgy mementoes
Of that other world as vague as doom
Looming and fading on mirages of skyline.

Volcanoes are understandable, blowing their tops,
Ejaculating lava like manly gods.
But — too close, too many, too big
(Our current nightmares) . . . That these should also

Weigh on mountains for millions of years,
That such tensions, like headaches, should leave seams
In mindless brows . . . Slates are like petrified
Sweatings of matter's neurosis.

TOWN AND COUNTRY

People who live in towns
Often talk to themselves.
They have little sunlight,
Less quiet, and nothing very fresh to eat.
Loving is quite a problem.

Their pleasures are not all that pleasant,
Though they pay dearly for them.
In a dry summer
Towns smell of money going bad.

Country people have skins like fruit, and vote like grandad.
They treat cattle like cows,
And speak kindly to strangers —
Though they use too many poisons
Which they buy from towns.

Suburban people are different from either,
Bringing up their gardens.
They are kind by committee,
And smile behind gates.
They are not seen talking to themselves.

Town people try very hard
Not to be taken in.
Sometimes they die of not being taken in
Anywhere by anyone.

The sky grows closer,

The landlords more so.
Chimneys get cleaner,
Green belts blacker.

HOLY COW

Should we pity or imitate —
As our beaten or better selves —
The graminivorous ruminants?

Who developed the poetic knack
Of snatching a bite on the run —
Having no surer defence
Than inglorious thin legs —
And chewing it over later.

Not that it got them far,
Except to keep them alive —
If you can call it a life,
Gormlessly jawing in clover,
Dreadfully mooing in sidings,
Crazy as all get out.

Look out. Here they come again,
The lions and flies, the hunters,
The businessmen, farmers and showmen,
Economists, chemists, castrators,
And the humane killers.
Run, you poor devils.
No use. Stay as you are.

We shall never leave you alone.
And your future's tied up with ours.
Born to be bullied and cowed,
More stomach for chewing than fighting,
Not preying on others. Being tapped.

Feeding snakes, hedgehogs and babies
As well as and more than your own,
And (as a professor once noted)
Meekly inheriting the earth.

THREE

Gifts, wishes, wise men, wise
Sayings of the Welsh, come in threes.
Shrines stood at the meeting of three ways.

Why weave a circle thrice?
What was three's charm? Why Trinity's
Balancing act above the skies?

Who first saw the threeness of three?
As potent a discovery
As fire or the axle tree.

(Triangles for apprehending land's
Unclimbable heights. Tripod's stance.
Triumvirs. And today the treble chance.)

Count three for its own sake,
Not as one of the many that can make
One and Many such a headache

For thinkers trying to endure
The cosmic smash and its litter
Flying further and further from the centre.

Two is worse: time's unhealer;
Poles' pull; pain's either/or;
Curls of chopped worm, him and her;

Ahriman and Ormuzd tied

To agreeing for ever to divide
Our world of outside and inside.

Oh but the human peace of three,
Not resolving magically
But still leaving a way

Out of becoming one all alone,
Or two agonising to make one.
Three is dimensional one.

Its charm is identity.
Say, I am one of three;
Therefore I must be.

WATER UNDER FOOT

Dowsers (who work rather like poets)
Apprehend a secret life of water
Under old magical sites. Plumb beneath
Stonehenge a buried spring surges,
Streams concur. As though holy men should
Walk on water, and the Just City
Floated or very faintly pulsed
In a rhythm like breathing or sucking.

                                      Now
The water table falls. Grunting wells
Grind harder deeper. In mountain bogs
As rich as molasses, boots
Sink lovingly, step leadenly
On terra firma paved with
Desperately good intentions. Our anchors
Bite hardcore. Subsidences whisper
Dryly. Some last mysterious freshets
Sprout through motorways after freak storms.

JANET HARRISON

THE GREAT BONE SHOW

Time is kind to bone
cleaning with intimate care
showing honeycombs of stone.

Bones ride our flesh,
by their strange struts
move us.

Self's hidden statue, buried shell
claims us kin to limestone, chalk
fragments of the hills we walk.

At our start limbs fold like fans
in bird-thin, rabbit-small
fretworks of ivory

which, catching flesh in their snug
burrow, float filigree as fish
in the quiet sea of their beginning.

A wind through straw bones
blows an egg-shell dome
fills it with brain, fanciful.

Away we stride
swaggering our bones as they grow;
but Time cries, 'Show, show.'

TAKING THE GOLDEN KEY FROM THE GLASS TABLE

Coming to Earls Barton
on a raw winter's morning,
the sun like skimmed milk

poured on the old tower,
I gaze at stone strip-work
lacing the walls, crude pillars
propping five Saxon arches.

Like Alice I find curious doors:
those set ladder-high, an exit on air,
one diminutive in the nave, eye-level,
another strangely low and narrow
set stark in the long stone wall.
What would I see if humbly small,
or in high spirits, I dared to open them?

The west door studded row on row
by nails, guards history in chevron
in the shadow of the worn arch.
What darkness lies the other side?
I would not venture that way;
Time rings a relentless chime
from that aloof and staggering belfry.

But those mysterious inner doors
let me open, let me kneel
like a child again and see, suddenly,
that first garden, radiant,
where a naked man and woman
walk by cool fountains talking
with Love in the evening light.

MEMORY ASKS

Did I run across the lawn
to stir with small feet
heaps of copper-beech leaves?

    I hear the rustle

see the gold-red turning
but the tree has gone.

Did I sing in a child's light voice
(the window-seat cold through my night-gown)
'Shenandoah' for my brother going to war?

    After six years a stranger came,
    I noticed only the mole on his nose;
    he called me by my first name.

Were there always shadows
of chestnut leaves flickering
on the bedroom ceiling?

    Always — winters pass;
    summer, like longing,
    stays in the mind.

Was there a rooster next-door
ruffled, fierce, six feet tall
who chased like a stabbing wind?

    That rooster is old age, illness,
    friends harried away
    by the long wind called death.

Was the dairy always cool
trickling with water and the cellar
a mossed cave for witches?

    Yes, water calms and fascinates,
    and the witch, like an old sheepdog
    came up and bit me through the lip.

A TIGER THINKS

four plump children into the air
(clutching school-bags, eyes startled)
to crown his pensive head.

In his striped mind
he cages them, brands
with bars set burning
in the forests of his night.

A richly savoured
shadow of thinking rustles
them, like gnats in a fall
of sunlight, to his jaws.

Grunting he turns trophy
slumps in a rug-like release
of sleep on warm concrete;
the children step down, meekly,
skip off to the monkey-house.

A GEOLOGIST SPEAKS STRANGELY OF BAUGHMAN'S SPRING

Peering at rocks, searching for garnets:
traces of red, shining like silica,
I was astonished in that mountain silence
to hear voices babbling behind me
sounding through the stillness
with a musical accompaniment.
Who would believe a flutter of angels
hovering thirty feet above the ground
and glittering – near Route 3?

My city ears were deaf to miracles,

my glass draws out the truth of stone,
and though I had been forty days
in those deserted places, tapping
the earth's veins with a small hammer,
I did not expect that spring
of sound to gush into my ears,
or such a glory of light to strike
from aspen leaves by the small stream.

BEYOND BELIEF

'Kiss me' said the frog to the princess
'and I'll turn into a handsome prince.'
Maybe she did and he didn't
or she didn't and he did —
caring is possible beyond all belief.
Consider the frogs on the bus
and the princess coming out
of that hardware shop,
or the 'Lovers In A Garden'
embroidered on an early carpet
by Zeruah Higley Guernsey Caswell.
Observe the magic of loving ugliness,
the care so stitched in time
to give us whey-faced figures:
he no neck, a blob in blue,
she knot-haired, a tea-pot lid
above the tight mouth, severe face.
He holds her wrist vice-like in his ardour
extends a boneless arm to point the way
he'll force her, Cinderella's sister,
beyond that formal potted plant
into their Eden. Could he
in his frog head really love her?
But 'yes' she says, and handsomely he does.

BEYOND THE SCOPE OF INSTRUCTION

In the sterile morning light
the class gathers, wrenched from sleep,
dropping books, shuffling into place.

Their glazed eyes turn towards me,
worry etches lines as they await
their transformation into writers.

'Be a kaleidoscope!' I thunder
in the silence
before my first words.

'Be a kaleidoscope' I whisper
gently, over their bent heads
as they score their notebooks.

'Be a kaleidoscope' I croon
to their awkward elbows
and sprawled, adolescent legs.

'Be a kaleidoscope' I dance
out-leaping Nijinsky
as I walk to the blackboard.

    I write:
Clear your eyes and focus
on everything, turning
the slow funnel of your memory
to scan each detail
scattered at your feet.
Peer through your singular mind
and marvel at its power
to cluster and pattern.
Plunge through interior mirrors

into another world, surreal
and half dark. Find
in your shaping spirit
an urge to capture and train
words, floating them down
the kaleidoscope of yourself
until, one day, they settle
graciously folding their wings
to stagger you utterly
by their beauty.

ON FINDING A PRINTED MESSAGE IN MY NEW BOOTS

Virginia Cline
of Wolverine World Wide
how grateful are our feet
that you have messaged them
so tenderly.

We're moved by all your hope,
and, yes, we find much comfort
in the durability, and still enjoy
that quality, stepping smartly out
of Rockford, Michigan
four-nine-three, four-one.

To think that you inspected
each portion of these boots,
felt out their uppers
peered beneath their zips
and rapped severely on each buckle,
makes us spring more lightly
through the winter's slush.

And so we stamp our pleasure

upon these chill and distant days
and write to say we're feeling fine
thanks much to you, Virginia Cline.

HAVEN'T YOU MET ME SOMEWHERE BEFORE?

I have nowhere to go
except, classically,
out of my mind.

I think I shall ride out
of this life in a small car.

Maybe I shall mouth
furies from closed windows
my head a medusa at the windshield
stoning the dog-strollers;
my hair writhes and writhes.

I croon a siren song
to the built-in radio.
Cars on the freeways
flock round me as I preen,
perched high for the razzle-dazzle,
a harpy, clawing the wheel.

Blocking the traffic
on a narrow off-ramp,
I bark human atrocities
from six heads and wink
my red green eyes, snarling
cars and trailers and even
airport buses towards
my oily chops;

or I lead them
swirling, swirling
over and under, loopy,
on some unlucky cloverleaf
dragging them like flotsam
at eighty and all brakes gone
jettisoned for my bright hair.

From these sad straits
I lure survivors
by soft shoulders
to concrete islands
promising hamburgers
pop-corn, candy and ice-cream.
See them gobble, gobble!

I shall drive out, flashing the red lights
of my mind, sucking the whole world
into my rear-view mirror.

TOWER OF BABEL

Look at that tree!

   Is it not a Port Orford Cedar?

No, do not name it —
Behold, a dark green tongue of flame
rises in a prayer to God.

   But I see the roots
   set in correctly cut ditch
   to hold its daily water.

Listen, can't you hear the voices,
in a multiplicity of holy sound, sing praises
above the valley of shadows?

I noticed a mocking-bird
and several finches fly in;
are those jays screeching?

Ah, heralding Advent they perch revealed
their colours gleam in the darkness,
angels flutter in that tree.

Do you expect small doors to open
like cuckoo-clocks, ticking off the Sundays
to Christmas, as if a tinsel calendar?

Only hear that splendour
how each ferned branching
seems to speak of sudden joy.

Of course I like to hear the birds
babbling cheerfully during a lull
in the traffic, but joy. . .?

I do not understand you.

THE MOVEMENT LESSON

The old professors look askance
at the young women, liberated,
unbound like new feet out of China.

'They'll rue it when they're forty'
says the Dean, sagely, watching them,
carefully bland and irreproachable.

They pass with a fine movement
of breasts convulsing their vibrant sweaters;
'I love it, love it' breathes the young instructor.

BIP

'What does he live on? Parsley? Electricity?' From a review of Marcel Marceau, *The Listener*, 3 August, 1972.

I

After the great bowls of parsley,
an ambrosial salad springing
the marrow of his limbs,
comes the slow sip at a crystal goblet
brimming with electricity.
What else can he feed on?

He splinters white from primal darkness;
his paradox gnaws at the knot of each heart:
suddenly Pentecostal strangely we talk
out of his silence, and at last
we understand.

He skips on an empty stage
and we are young again
chasing the butterflies that hover
at his fingertips and our senses
flutter new-fledged and sing over
his head; his eyes follow like larks.

Candle-flame leaning in a draught,
this tremulous form makes
out of emptiness, a cage, like life
forcing him inward and inward; then unmakes
steel walls in the blink of our eyes
letting us breathe again, as we step,
shaken as the flower in his top hat,
to our freedom.

II

Poet of all clowns, you perform

the dancer *and* the dance;
we know each David and Goliath
stoning and storming within us,
each sin personable, rollicking or mean
squatting at the head, heart or belly.

Illusive before our spell-bound eyes
which wholly believe you Merlin,
we watch those raw ingredients
mix their magic as you suggest
the mundane rabbit, that old hat. . . .

Feet drum the stage!
A hundred white tails scud
from your ferreting, sinuous hands
and your excessive smile rises
V-shaped above our applause
as the theatre leaps alive
and a scent of creatures
fills the fleeting air.

TROGLODYTES TROGLODYTES

Farthing bird
how can you be
four inches long
when you are only
round like the full-stop
to your tail's exclamation?

Brown mouse, running
along the wall, suddenly
you hurl off in a gale
thistle-down bob to the high-wire,
a minute clown swinging under
as I crowd at the window, laughing.

Late spring I hear you
all voice-box, a feathered note
calling three brown dots,
extensions of your trill,
to follow, louder than size
fast as flung nutmegs.

DUSK FOLK

Haven't you seen them
advancing across a summer field
in the almost dark
smelling of dried clover, sweet grasses?

The dog turns
barking; the rough of his nape
stirs as he sniffs
the warm wind.

Then he comes close
to my heels, only glancing
opal eyes their way
as I watch them lean

out of the twilight —
curious, maybe,
in their tall, dark throng
stopped always to watch

us. Yet rustling forward —
moths lifting from under
their long clothes, which sway
slightly in the wind —

whenever we move. Their faces
blend into shadow;

I can only imagine
the ancient features

gnarled or wrinkled as apples,
the veins on hidden hands
like leaves fading to skeletons,
the hair shaggy as grass or straw.

They press after me,
whispering at hay-warm dusk
of some deep kinship
I no longer recall.

TO THE CONTRARY

Each of us
harbours doves and crocodiles:
some great dramatic double face
of peace and rage.

The mood may settle lightly
begin to preen each comely feather,
the eye brilliant
above such softness. . . .

When a sudden stir will stretch us
darkly heavy, to snap and flail,
dangerous jawed, our leather armour
ready to avert spears.

See how one flutters down
to the quiet pool, a pearl in moss,
only surprised when the reflection
dips a long snout, turns to the attack.

Metamorphosis comes from the gods.

Let each, heraldic, claim his bestiary
and find his moods a rich perplexity.
I hail the monstrous dove behind your eyes.

DEATH ON THE FARM

Ay Sue, you may well turn pale
you can tell from our faces
the news is bad, or did you see
him coming feet first and useless
past the window – your Thomas?

Now, hold my hand, sit on the bench,
put your arm round the lass
your eldest, already weeping for him
put down like a log, jaw slack. He's gone
your husband. How to feed six children

strikes quick on your loving sorrow
for Thomas Drake dead, who laboured
all his life from a lad of seven
on the Turnill's farm, kept you all
best as he could in the damp cottage;

struggled through these bad times:
warrants filching land from us poor
who grubbed a little extra there.
We'll remember his wrestling too
the falls others took at Michaelmas Fair.

Somehow he slipped. The horse moved?
Sheaves not set right on the wagon?
He fell. His neck broke.
We couldn't move for fear;
only the scribbling lad of Helpston
fell down in a fit, that young John Clare.

I'D KNOW HER ANY TIME

Strange to meet her in this posture
with the face of a modern girl:
wide brown eyes, dark hair
pulled back behind her ears
and falling shawl-like
on her shoulders,
the face a little pinched
or unresponsive.

Meet her anywhere in London;
see her on the bus in town.

Now the face stares back
across the years,
her coverlet arrayed in gods
and mourners, sons of Horus,
Nile plants, the vulture-goddess
hovering on blue-black wings
like death's own bruise.

Only her feet,
this final bed too short,
stick out beyond a fringe,
the emblematic cover
hitched too high, as if her night
were long, or restless;

her end marks time:
twelve toes so oddly even
stay present in my mind.

CAROL FOR OUR CHERRY TREE

The young men rode in, apostle-like and gentle,
beards lifted on the wind, machines glittering light.

'Then Mary said to Joseph, so meek and so mild,
"Joseph gather me some cherries, for I am with child."

The young women met them, arms circled with rope,
faces rosy from frost in a garden bleakly winter.

Then Joseph flew in anger, in anger flew he,
"Let the father of the baby gather cherries for thee."

Young men drew the cross-cut sharp into the bark,
young women roped branches, snaring this wild-bird.

Then Jesus spoke a few words, a few words spake he,
"Give my mother some cherries, bow down cherry tree."

The tree shook from the sky, stark boughs clattering
fell heavy on the lawn, life cut before New Year.

"Bow down, O cherry tree, low down to the ground."
Then Mary gathered cherries and Joseph stood around.'

The young folk linked arms and lifted up the tree,
wood fine for carving, the grain like melody.

PHILIP CRICK

THE ADMAN COMETH

he taketh our hearts
he stitcheth each up
he stealeth our mind
encloseth our thought
he filleth us with longing for the true product

he probeth our psyche
he knoweth desire
and how to appease,
he loveth our gold
he lifteth our purse
he coaxeth clear coin from our wondering hand

the adman cometh
and sootheth our hurt

the adman
    cometh

        legal and clean

           the bastard.

MINIPOEM

One hot blue noon
in the suburb of Somewhere
passing a girl
of six green summers, I
suddenly said:

there is a byelaw
penalty
of 5 pounds

should your puppydog foul
the footway

to which she answered
unhesitatingly:
I
like
my
sunhat.

SLIPSTREAM

At flood-tide, the current
is glass, an immaculate rift; Thames
a chasm of light.

On the flickering bank
men walk the raft
of a wafer-thin world; river

And anti-river fight
and the flanking trees are hurled
up from their quaking roots.

Fish in the wind
a single seagull drives
over the strict abyss;

Bird of the stream
his matching phantom slides
under descending sky.

MOLLUSC

The dialogue
of rain with light
born of the systole
of the moon
is what I know
is what I own.

I have no soul.
I live by rote.
Around my cone
a horizontal tumult rides
Within me: chemistry
and calm, and fate.

High up, white shapes
breed wings, transform.
I hear their bleak
flesh-haunted cry.
In opal space
they wheel like snow.
They scour the chaos
of the sky.

Not I. Not I.
I am content
to fix, to spawn,
unendingly to multiply.

They scour the chaos of the sky;
But who can match
my faithful mind?
Engraved on rock
my jujube eye
confronts its truth
All movement kills,
Desire is blind.

In my cool tent
no passion swills.
Foe of the loose
provocative sea,
I camp among
my steadfast kind.

PERSIAN LOVE-LILT

Cats
are creeps
cats preside, they
crouch
they gaze, they say
nothing, their thoughts
are bare
and exact
and photos.

Cats trap sounds
outside our hearing,
they are thermotropic, they
understand heat.

Cats make love
in a strangled kind of Urdu
their passions
provoke us, and draw
water.
Cats
have boats
inside their throats
but their paws
are sexy.

Cats
were gods
but have given up.
There are no exams
or diplomas for cats,
they are hooked
on sleep
and processed
whales.

Cats do yoga
but so
do dogs.

PRISON SONG

Sky, my unfamiliar,
I creep fettered
in your blue cell, dank
with rain, and heavy-fruited stars.

I have grasped your codes,
mastered your deep routine, become
a model prisoner.

Once, in fear
I pressed my nose
against your peerless glass; no blood
sprang, no bruise rose. No voice
appeased my questioning.

Your punishment
was silence.

OPPOSITIONS

Up the tame end
the lawn is fascist, measured
and formal,
kind to the dream, conducive to golf
and the opulent
lilo.

And the roses, the roses
loll in their clusters, their cream formations
shaped by romance
to the wanderer's will.

In such a clear enclave
lager is proper,
the ice-cube may shimmer
beneath a fat lily.
     The chat
is of Africa
(in cultivated rhythms)
of impenitent children
and war in the street.

But down at the wild end
the dumbness is total.
Only high poppies
lithe on their stem
ejaculate blood from the shattered blue pod.

Only the rumour
of sunflower chaos,
crisis and woodsmoke, vipers
of crimson;

And under heaped ash
a fang of sour gold.

QUASI-HAIKU

1. An enormous cat roams through our sleep.
   Its deep fur hisses in the rainsoaked leaves.
   Half-roused we hear, on dark horizons
   its purring join the pulse of trains.

2. Power scream the pines
   in the demonstrating forest;

   Grey banners of rain appease their cry.

3. In tones of apricot and umber
   trees predict the coming sleep.

   By flooded lawns the sunflowers hang their chins
   and speak of shadow.

4. Deference is the sickening twin of Command
   and neither should be trusted.

5. The middleclass tulip prizes her bed.
   The giant orchid holds court in the suntrap.

   Only the roughcut dandelion
   professes global rights.

6. Blessed are the speechmakers
   for they shall inherit
   the clap.

7. There are more stanzas in the volume of the sea
   than have ever clambered out of it.

8. I see mankind as a fuzzy slide
    of an orphaned wingless moping bird
    projected in error by an amateur god
    right to left, and upside down.

9. It is easier to walk through the eye of a thrush
    than to swim the Charing Cross Road.

10. Opportunity never
    simply knocks. It flutters
    a wing twice, then
    vanishes, like a hummingbird.

11. It was the sort of day when two young lovers
    could halt in the traffic and blocking out mankind
    swallow each other's hearts.

12. The innovating sun
    clings
    to her skin; those legs, that
    prance, that high
    untaken look!
    At 50 mph I crash into my future.

13. Mechanical doors in me
    unfold at once when you stand near.
    Aroused I purr
    ready to flash you anywhere.

    How can I though, when we see that the route
    is published already, each fare stage fixed?

FANTASIA ON A THEME OF WAR

Tanks ring town.
Our frenzy is to win,
and then, to keep on winning.
The doves are all shot down.

In this abandoned land
the army is perpetual.
No captain or his men
can even now remember
how, by whom, or when
the last campaign began.

Crashing on in teams
across gold miles of grain,
you and I are gunners
unafraid of pain;
yet always we go planning
ladders of desire
deep inside our dreams.

Hearing small-arms rain
we swop a veteran stare.
Freedom or revenge
our enemies prepare,
and IBMs exchange
under the horizon.

Now distant bombs abuse
the soundless shape of hills;
Now dead men must acquire
that which dead men lose,
and sleepwalk on, as conquerors.

Our corporals uncork booze;
but you let drop your pack
and gulp down hoarded wine.

You joke that I'm okay
(not like those other swine)
And I joke back, and watch
a skylark hurl from corn.

She floats where we would be.
She tells how love was born.
Who gave the sky this pearl?
We track her shrilling speck
above these farms of murder.

FABLE

As you slept, and snored
a shock-battalion roared
among the streets of home.
Their skidding half-tracks clawed
the upland of your dream.
And though you could not rouse
to parry their attack
you cried out loud just once
then sank below the storm.
Shouts, you can remember
and sliding shadows, tall
with undetermined fear; a sword
blade severing corn.

In this reviving dawn
you breakfast unaware
that some great war has gone
since you last lived and sang;
that spiders camp in the hessian
and all that can remain
is monuments, medallions,
mean pensions for the brave,
the tensions of the widow,

the bombscare of the slave,

the amnesia of the general,
wrapped in his maps, and power;
the stalemate of the treaty,
the checkmate of the funeral;

and that red mourning flower
alive on the windowpane;
the scarecrow and its cockerel
crossbreeding on the plain.

MARIONETTE

Chimes from a spire, at six,
and soon, the drum of clocks.
The noise floats every black rook home
in glum, freewheeling sparks.

Sport of sex and science,
of trade, and tax, and gun,
I feel their worried wire
hawser through my thumb.

The sky is a forest fire,
but pylons pierce its glory;
God, in his padded room,
has hammered out my story.

Marionette, I'm drawn
to the gag, to the gig, to talk.
Woodentop, I gape
totter from the sheet, then walk.

Unsold tortoises don't sing, don't bark,
dumbness their one vocation, the
loose crêpe skin sewn upon the dark
aboriginal tub of a spine, the small
animal soul boxed in, the red valve of a heart
entombed, inaudible. No
dusky arabesque of thighs, or dance
of paws. Slow instead,
on canny claws, the four
begrudging stodgy thumbs advance.

And more surprise;
each one of such impure, bizarre
students of Diogenes
can telescope at whim, can render or withdraw
on scrawny neck, the razor ridge of jaw
the glossy miser's nose, and empty
influenzal eyes, which parody
a judge's introspective gaze
of wise emaciation.

Obscure, opaque, inscrutable,
through force of mounded mass
and convoluted shape, intriguing to the touch,
these trustees of geology
these hummocks in the sawdust
of the seed-and-sparrow shop
directionless as dodgems, tap
the frosted glass, upturn, or sleep
overwhelmed by apathy.

But should by chance an inmate creep
beyond this trap, and purchased, fall
to harbour near a garden fence,
some stark eruption of the soul
ennobles him;

Gigantic suns from antique dawns
that shook the fronded, blind
foreshores of green infancy
spiral through his crooked mind.

Disowning now, the cosy hell
of sympathy and nourishment
that strangled him, he bolts from commonsense, and heaves
columbuswise his cumbrous ship
of rippled shell
away to Eldorado.

ECHO CHAMBER

Two mirrors now confront
reflect a twin retreat
of endless tinier oval.

How may the light-wave pass
crash rebound and dive
into the convex glass,
torrent of total calm
and cold reverberation?

Through such enchanted holes
the sun, from hour to hour
disposes all its children.

MY CROOKED MOTHER

who loved no-one, who
gibed at her blood, who soured her own lungs
in a flood of pride, who
orphaned my heart from her dextrous fingers;
my crooked mother, my crooked
crooked mother, stubborn as stone, who slowly fed
the roving, ten-fanged ferret of pain
in her knees, in her knuckles
in her shuddering
side

is lying prone
is an image of wax on a smooth glass bed
immersed in the healing of her endless absence.

PURE KNOWLEDGE

Can mirrors grip their images?
or a sky
examine blue?

That which touches that which is touched
finds meaning only
                        in the severance of caress.

QUIBERON

A ten-ton man
in a suit of stone
dozes face down
on the edge of France.

His green jaws nudge
the immaculate beach
and the low waves lance
a rift in his bone.

All ropes unreel
in his waterlogged heart.
He sways on his bed.
His vertebrae moan.

And he floats a long cry
down through the sand
that even the stars
and the quasars own.

Its echo shatters
the sky off Belle-Ile.
At sunset, too,
sea-owls murmur.

PROGENY

They ripple round his years, assiduous as vine
and meshed in merriment mock
his tumbled spiky crown.

His scheming taproot dies, his dozen sinews knock
each arcing sun in fear
then weep as it burns down.

But they leap onward clear
(slim tendrils in green eyes)
caprice, dance, immediacy, the motif of their being.

HOME NEWS

A grey-red parrot
flashed through our house,
and a squirrel bought out
our cherrytree.

These are not omens
or signals
or signs,
or the substance of some homily.

But data, data
delightful
data.